before after

OWEN MCLEOD

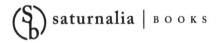 saturnalia | BOOKS

Distributed by Independent Publishers Group
Chicago

Saturnalia Books
105 Woodside Rd.
Ardmore, PA 19003
info@saturnaliabooks.com

ISBN: 978-1-947817-52-4 (print), 978-1-947817-53-1 (ebook)
Library of Congress Control Number: 2022947290

Cover art and book design by Robin Vuchnich

Distributed by:
Independent Publishing Group
814 N. Franklin St.
Chicago, IL 60610
800-888-4741

Contents

Before

After

Before

The Owen McLeod Poet Action Figure

is now available in select retail outlets,
the sort you can find in those dying malls
not far from the regional airport. I come
with a set of miniature accessories: desk,
laptop, fridge, and toilet, plus a rusted-out
Honda Civic. My limbs bend in such a way
that you can slump me behind the laptop,
staring into nothingness, or park me in front
of the open fridge, contemplating emptiness.
If you're 18 years or older, try planting me
in front of the toilet, hunched, so I can jack off
over the bowl. After that's done, fold me
into the Civic, as if I'm going somewhere,
but bend my body forward until my head
rests gently on the steering wheel. Keep me
in that pose for about five or ten minutes
then reposition me behind the laptop.
If that doesn't sound like fun, you could
rip off my head and replace it with Barbie's
or strap a pack of firecrackers to my chest
and blow me to smithereens in the backyard,
or squash me into a fetal ball and bury me alive
in the sandbox. I know, I know: you outgrew
action figures a long time ago. That's cool.
The Owen McLeod Poet Action Figure
is OK with languishing in the bargain bin,
lodged between discontinued rawhide chews

and last summer's glow-in-the-dark Frisbees.
Someday, someone will scoop me up and find
the secret button, no bigger than a pinhead,
concealed in the sole of my foot, or under
a patch of my thinning hair. If you press it
just right, and hold me tight against your heart,
I'll whisper the words *You are infinitely precious.*
You are loved and you belong. You are stronger,
more beautiful, than even God could know.

Thief

Every Thursday, on his way to therapy,
he drives past the house of the woman
he's having an affair with. What interests
his therapist isn't the sin, which she views
as a symptom, but the root. So they dig,
or seem to, and today he talks about his wife—
how, before they take a trip, she makes him
connect those timers to lamps in certain rooms,
and how much this annoys him, even though
it didn't used to. As if their belongings were
of value. As if an automatic light might stop
an addict from breaking in.
                              As if the thief,
awake beside her, had not already been.

In the Credit Union Lobby

I want to be happy—
here, seated in a plastic chair, reading
in *Field & Stream* the story of Jason,

a bilateral amputee
who, through hard work, taught himself
to hunt again—

or, if not happy, then at least
not unhappy. If Jason can come back
from losing both arms below the elbow,

surely I can survive
First Commonwealth Federal Credit Union
and my meeting with Meghan,

the mortgage loan officer
who will finalize certain matters
related to the divorce.

I wanted to be happy,
there on the rain-soaked driveway,
hugging the last box of your belongings.

People lose these things all the time:
marriages, homes. Nothing
compared to losing two limbs.

In an image from the magazine, Jason
hoists the head of the ten-point buck
he shot in the woods of Kentucky.

This is a picture of what it takes
to be happy: cradling in your arms
the thing that you killed.

MARK 6:11

This morning Christ texts me
from the cross, not in words
but in an indecipherable string

of emojis: scorpion birthday cake
Easter Island statue pushpin radar
stiletto heel Chinese flag umbrella.

Lord, please let me be. He replies
with toilet panda plus animated gif
of Oprah repeatedly squinting.

Sometimes I wake up, wrong
bunk, wrong crew, ship locked
in an ocean of ice. Days like that

I stay in my sweats, watch clips
of soldiers reuniting with their pets,
weep, or half-heartedly meditate.

At 33, I spent six months
in a monastery in Chiang Mai,
seeking my Buddha nature.

The most beautiful woman
I ever knew wasn't beautiful
when I looked inside her room.

I used to pray for good signs:
flexing arm, trophy, clapping hands,
smiley face with hearts for eyes,

but all I get is briefcase kimono gun
downward arrow eight-ball alligator pill.
Jesus once instructed the disciples

to shake the dust from their sandals
on their way out of any town
that failed to hear the gospel.

In the corners of my house,
on each counter and shelf, dust
so thick you could write my name.

EAGLE BEACH

After promises, he's invited
to his younger sister's house,
a cabin on a mountain lake.

For three days, he sips seltzer
with wedges of lemon or lime,
but on day four, he steals away,

hikes the half-mile driveway,
and drinks the fifth he stashed
among thistles on his way in.

When he returns, hours later,
he is given a day to sober up
before being asked to leave.

Sometimes he closes his eyes
and tries to will himself back:
napping on the dock, reading

to his niece, talking to his sister
while she slices fresh peaches
in the peace of her sunlit kitchen.

She tried, on the lake, to teach him
how to float. Breathe, she said.
Let the water hold you up.

A Sonnet on My Birthday

This morning I scan the news on my phone,
eat one boiled egg and a piece of dry toast,
drink a pot of coffee, do two loads of clothes.
I keep making the same mistakes: confusing love
with infatuation, blaming people not situations,
inflicting my worst self on my dearest friends,
taking everything good for granted, projecting
what's corrupt in me onto the innocent world,
clinging to dust, ignoring the moon and stars.
Along the river, partly frozen in this season,
seagulls huddle atop the warehouse roofs
in vast, steaming flocks. Why are they here, far
from any sea, squabbling over scraps of litter?
I'm fifty-two today. I pray for thirty more years.

Portrait of Woman with Cabbages

You loved her limousine legs, breadbox heart,
her zip code, her report card red with wrong,
the way she'd curl up in your sleeping bag,
mix her elixirs, adjust the dials, plug in
to the weird sprawling world hovering
just above her head like a helium slum.
Her laugh was money for the Laundromat.

It happened gradually, then suddenly.
She identified faces on the kitchen floor,
mostly friendly at first, mostly human,
but increasingly neither. Her theories multiplied:
data ladders, the secret constitution of things,
invisible contaminants, black forces, voices.

By then, it was too late. You'd started
a small farm together, trying to grow
organic vegetables. One day she said
that certain forms of dust could wreck
the workings, that the greens would decay,
that we'd have to take corrective action.

How do you stop someone from suffocating
a vegetable garden with black plastic tarp?
You can't mention photosynthesis, because
the sun has become irrelevant. Suddenly
there are two realities, two loves, or rather
two ways of loving. You must choose one.

The last time you saw her, she was in there.
You walked together in the shadow of that place.
Dull with pills, jump-started like a stalled car,
she said the thread from which we all hang
is a noose. You flapped your dumbass wings,
not knowing what else to do. She laughed
as you flew, her old Laundromat laugh. Coins fell
through the holes in your pockets like rain.

Breakup at the Starfish Brasserie

I imagine myself as the simplified figure
in your future and falsified romantic idea
of the present. You claim you've stopped
believing in a point where sculptures end
and furniture begins. Well, bully for you
is all I can say—that, and have a good one.

The sad thing is that there *is* more than one
way to skin our cat. Add the dog, I figure
it's thirty-nine ways in total. Of course, you
don't actually skin them. That's not the idea.
The truth is that there's no beginning or end
to anything—or so you'd say, if not stopped.

Do you remember the weekend we stopped
talking to each other? That was definitely one
of the loudest times in our lives. The end
was near, but not near enough for us to figure
that out. I'll admit, it was an interesting idea
for me to call you me and you to call me you,

as if this inversion might save me and you
from extinction. It was fun until it stopped
being fun, which was when I had the idea
that we are two distinct people, not one
person in two bodies. Certainly my figure
was different from yours, especially at the end,

when I was overweight, a blob at the end
of the bar. "The body is the soul," you
said, but I was too damn drunk to figure
out what you meant. Eventually I stopped
trying. "Here's to one for all and all for one!"
We clinked our glasses to a dumb idea.

Meanwhile, in Canada, geese get the idea:
It's time to start heading south. The end
of things is clear to them: summer is one
season, winter another. They're not like you
and me, muddling everything. If they stopped
to think, they'd fall from the sky. Go figure.

In the parking lot, we stopped loving even the idea
of each other. I figure it was an appropriate end:
that honk, above, from one lost goose. That was me—and you.

Saturday Morning

The sky looks nothing like a Turner painting
and a crocodile snaps at the bottom of the stairs
while devices I don't understand bleat the blowing
of arms and legs off children in parts of the world
I don't know but know I feel I should.

Never mind all that. Silence your phone and hide
with me among the blue pillows in the beautiful
machine that eats your velvet scrunchies. If we hurry
we can cram our love between the time it is now
and the moment before the milk expires.

Mission accomplished, pal. Let me tell you
what a time we had, but right now we're on our way
to the farmer's market on foot. Sort of a ritual
with us, a way of getting back to their idea of our idea
of Eden and away from these suffocating units.

On the hot walk home we rest on a bench beside
the river and remember Mr. Pibb. We talk again
about having children but come to no decision.
A yard sale sucks us in. We solemnly file past a shoebox full
of the limbless figures Fisher-Price calls People.

ENTOMOLOGY

Once upon a time you drew The True
on a napkin from the Iron Horse Music Hall.
You knew more than I about *Being & Time*,
plus a bunch of other stuff, like where
to salvage sinks they don't make anymore.

Month by month, I memorized your lines.
You burned a blue voice, scorched a rainfall wing,
arced many midnights on a turnip-white moon.
On Sundays, you'd fit in my hands like a bowl.
Your dials were marvelous. You stole my how.

I miss you half the time, always while reading
the *National Audubon Society Field Guide
to North American Insects & Spiders*.
Your pale green body with bright red stripes
was covered with yellowish wax.

I was totally cool with that, plus
the weird way you nudged me
until I stopped singing, devoured my body
while I transferred funds. In the morning
in the garden your cheetah was wow.

I think you might be anything by now:
otter, billboard, a temple of cement.
You're not what I thought you were, that's for sure,
not even the doll's head I found on the bus
on the long and lonely ride home.

Blood Vessels

I have been strange, I have been on pills,
I have been seen slumped against the pump,
gas gushing like lust from the tank. I've dug
with my hands a massive crater in the sand
just to watch the ocean rush in. So it's been:
draining one thing, filling another, sometimes
the same vessel, like the bottle polished off
halfway to Boston, then tossed piss-filled
from the Tappan Zee. Did I drive up north
to marry you? I remember the diner booth,
the spent capsules of cream, and your voice,
as if from the moon, explaining why the man
on your wedding cake would never be me.
I remember a hole appearing in the roof,
a rescue helicopter hovering overhead,
and the harness lowered down just for you.
I spent the rest of that night at a pub
somewhere in Somerville. I remember
a cloudy mirror above the bar, the stink
of the men's room, the sticky tiled floor,
and two young women making love in a stall—
one being emptied, the other being filled.

FRAGMENTS FROM THE GUMBALL SCROLLS

i had a rubber doll

                                        once it wasn't

rubber it wasn't

                         a doll i don't

                          remember who it was

                    once i had a loving

                                 mother she wasn't

                  loving she wasn't

my mother she was   a sex

                    worker

        i picked up after work

                                            sometimes

                    i had a girlfriend

once a girl she wasn't

                    a friend she wasn't

             they were

              a they i

          met at a gay bar

                      in detroit

                          i once stuck my thing

in a standard poodle it wasn't

                      my thing it was

              my head it wasn't

                      a standard poodle it was

              a gas oven

now i   live in the second circle
                      of hell it is not
                                  the second circle it is

a soggy taco
    bell bag stuck
in the storm
                                        drain

i used to believe in things
                i didn't believe in them
          they were not things but

now
                              i think about it
                    i mean really

stop & think about it
           maybe they were
& maybe

                          i hope
                 i did

Heart of Hearts

Car, plane, and train
to Sèvres, on the rumor
of a standard heart
with which I might
replace my own

red tumor. Platinum-
iridium alloy,
diamond hard, even harder
than history, a pump
for Plato's blood

this heart of should.
Elementary heist!
Nothing to it.
Even ideal hearts
are a cinch to steal.

Transplant's another matter.
Uncertain art,
swapping meat
for stainless archetype,
but the heart is made

for gambles.
And what was gained?
At best a break-even:
unbreakable spring, but too perfect
to love a thing.

CRATERS

The man drowned himself in Crater Lake,
the country's deepest at two thousand feet.
He didn't want to be recovered. (He wasn't.)
Before he left, he burned everything
in a bonfire: letters, clothing, pictures—
as if he'd never existed in the first place.

If you've ever had to clear out the house
of a dead man, you might say we were lucky.
But we didn't feel that way. We crawled
on our hands and knees over the rough planks
of his cabin floor, as if we were penitents
or pilgrims in the last stage of the journey.
We sought some trace of him, some ghost,
but found only walls and corners and rust.

After the others had given up and gone,
I got drunk, stepped out of my clothes
and slept in the ashes of what he'd torched
out back. I woke up under the moon, confused,
powdered in dust like the man up there. I knelt
at the pump, drew water from the deep, washed
in the light of his lakes and craters.

Yet Another Walk Away

Yet another walk away
from a freshly filled hole.
Some pray. Others wonder
if there's gum in the car.

She stops beneath a tree
and weeps for what she claims
are dying gods but look
like falling leaves to me.

Back home, machines worry
about the size of our load, ask
how we're feeling (delicate,
normal, or heavy duty), warn

of emergencies:
door is not locked, bucket
is full, filter needs changing,
batteries are low.

Some say there's a function
that takes these facts, banal
and mean, and somehow yields
a transcendental thing.

I woke with faith in that alchemy,
but tonight all I see
is a pair of rank vultures
hovering over the alphabet.

The machine on my lap
double-checks with me. Yes, I am sure
I want to quit Word. No, do not
remember me on this device.

REUNION

My elder sister sits on the back porch
as night falls. She smokes, nurses a beer,
and tells me stories about the man I knew
from old photographs, gone now too.
But this isn't about a bad father.
There's nothing left to say about him.
This is about my sister, now invisible
except for her ember. She remembers
when she was four and swore to him
she had a secret. Of course she had none,
but when he bent down to hear it, she bit
his ear hard enough to draw blood.
She laughs, now as then, at her act
of pre-revenge—but now she has two
ex-husbands, half-finished tattoos, a job
cleaning rooms in a Pensacola motel,
and secrets she doesn't tell me.

Bushkill Creek

On Bushkill Creek, a version of me meets me.
Everything's arranged, except for what to say
after thirty years. In the made-for-TV version,
there's a montage of father and son reunited
at last: reeling in the fish, lounging on the bank,
frying the day's catch over an intimate campfire.
In reality, I'm clueless about fishing. My father,
an old pro, has to loan me a pair of waders.
We slog out to the middle of the creek
that weaves through my town. I'm startled
by the water's depth, not to mention its chill.

Neither of us asks the only question to ask.
My father defaults to the language he knows—
mayflies, nymphs, the cunning of brown trout—
while I burn through half a dozen ill-fitting roles.
Nothing is caught. We split a cheese sandwich
on the tailgate of his truck. Suddenly, time is up.
My father asks for the best way to the interstate
so I sketch a map on a mustard-stained napkin.
We shake hands and mumble of meeting again.
A buzzard circles overhead, descends, then rises
and drifts away after seeing we're just two men.

Jaws

Among my elder sister's belongings,
I find an old tobacco tin.
Within, assorted teeth—
baby teeth, maybe hers, but adult teeth too,
too many to be hers, as well as teeth
from horses, deer, sharks, plus
many I can't identify. Spread out
on the bare mattress, they seem to come
from a single maw, horrible and huge,
belonging to the beast that consumed her—
as if, in the course of those final years,
what ruined her arms were these teeth that gnashed
as she tried to defang the thing.

Black Box

At 83, the end isn't
close enough to touch
but close enough to see—

like his mailbox out front,
black as a hearse,
waiting at the curb

with its red flag up.

BLUE CAMARO

I'm up at 6 a.m. to write, but all I do is stare
at the rain and the trees and watch the wind
strip away what remains of November's leaves.
Somewhere in Virginia, my father is dying.
Not on the sidewalk of a sudden heart attack
from shoveling snow, or in a hospital room
monitored by nurses and beeping machines,
but at home, alone, almost imperceptibly.
That man was never satisfied with anything.
When leaves were green he wanted them red,
when red then brown, when brown then fallen
and gone. One weekend, after raking them
into a curbside pile, he tossed in a cinderblock
meant for the local punk who'd been plowing
his 1982 Camaro through the heaped up leaves
of our neighborhood. Two days later, the kid
blew through our pile without suffering a scratch.
My father didn't realize that I, fearing for him
as much as for the boy, had fished out the brick
and chucked it in the ravine behind our house.
As punishment, I had to climb down in there,
retrieve the cinderblock, and bury it in the leaves
after I'd raked them back into a mound. My dad
said that was nothing if I dared to take it out.
I can still see him, stationed at the window,

watching and waiting for that boy to return—
but he never did, because I tipped him off
the next day after spotting him at the 7-Eleven.
Decades later and hundreds of miles away,
a malignant brick buried deep inside him,
my father waits again at the living room window,
listening for the rumble of that blue Camaro.

Sonnet to My Inheritance

Someone comes
for the gold, the car,
the house itself

but not the half-used
roll of plastic wrap,
the perfectly good

tube of toothpaste.
Taught not to waste,
I shove them

in a pillowcase.
For now, I'm safe
from the rot of death—

leftovers fresh,
minty clean breath.

VENDING MACHINE SUTRA

We stroll in the garden, admire
the irrigated Buddhas.

You carve a tiny coffin
from a scrap of soft pine.

Corpse headquarters,
you call it.

I wish for one like that,
a keychain casket—

next to it, at the funeral,
my colossal corpse

mocking the smallness,
the stinginess of death.

Meditation for Beginners

Sunrise spills its oranges on the street.
Birds go berserk in the leafed-out trees.
On mornings like these, he walks for miles
along a grassy trail beyond the cornfield,
his mind decomposing in multiple ways.
He worries mostly about his age, his failures
and obscurity, how events that at first seemed
accidental turned out to have been necessary—
nothing, in other words, worth writing down.
He prays for something like enlightenment,
then waits for it to arrive. Meanwhile, the days
become shorter and cooler, the sumac steadily
reddens, until the corn, grown impatient,
shrugs its shoulders and walks away.

Last Requests

I want to be excused, at least this once,
from being me, and by some miracle roll
over dams, under the bridges of cities,

a great green river neither believing
nor disbelieving, not searching or keeping,
always yet never the same thing, flowing.

I want a moment of silence for the girl
I secretly loved in high school, whose suicide note
was just a dog-eared J. Crew summer catalog.

She wrote poems with a leaky Bic pen,
skipped school to read novels
in the fruit-filled woods along the river.

I want as my final image, please,
her tapering fingers, blackened by ink,
plucking those wild persimmons.

My Life in Oz

I paid so much attention
to that man behind the curtain,

his furrowed brow,
the inscrutable gaze,

that I missed altogether
the curtain itself—

its emerald silk,
those tiny, embroidered roses.

Ricketts Creek

It's easy to say, "See things in such a way
that you become the thing you see,"
but hard to be the shriveled blue balloon

that somehow found its way into the woods.
Harder still to be the sunlight, hardest of all
the moon. On the long drive home, you try

to focus on what you're told—that happiness
should be sought in the soul, not the world—
but through the windshield you see a crow

picking at the guts of a possum squashed
in the road. What in the soul doesn't come
from the world, its dumpsters and coffins,

its cardboard and tin? How could the soul
be a cloud with a lid for lifting and finding
a pure self within? Burning with thirst,

you ease the pickup into roadside weeds.
There, reflected in a tainted stream, you cup
the heavens in your hands and drink.

How to Stop Yourself from Crying

From the side porch, you watch a cardinal gather material for the nest she's building in azaleas behind the garage.

You feel a lump in the pocket of your shirt. It's a nugget of cobalt blue glass.

Your sister texts you a picture of chocolate croissants fresh from her oven.

A UPS truck halts in front of the house across the street. The driver, in his cocoa-colored uniform, drops off a package near the front door.

The house belongs to a woman whose husband recently died. You attended the memorial service. Only afterwards, on the drive home, did you realize what you should have written in the book of remembrance.

You can't decide if you should reply to your sister with thumbs up, smiley face, or heart, so you just send all three.

The male cardinal arrives, but doesn't help his mate with the nest. Instead, he hops around in the mulch beneath the azaleas, hunting for small insects.

Holding the glass nugget to the sun, you remember finding it in the silt along the shore of the lake where your sister and her partner have a summerhouse.

You try to look at the male cardinal through the nugget, hoping the combination of cobalt and crimson will produce a purple cardinal, but the glass is too dark to see through.

The woman across the street steps out of her house. You think about waving and saying hello, but she quickly collects her package and disappears into the house.

You begin to feel the familiar sensation of wings sprouting from your shoulder blades. You never know what kind of wings they'll be.

You hope for violet cardinal-shaped wings, large enough for you to fly back in time to the memorial service and correct your entry in the book of remembrance.

But when the wings emerge, they're puny and olive-brown, just like the female cardinal's.

You text your sister a picture of your wings. She replies with a starry-eyed unicorn.

You begin to gather twigs for the nest.

After

The Host Will Let You in Soon

After a night spent high above the roof,
I descend with a revised system for civilization.
Those cold, distant mountains?
They're not why we're here.
I did learn something from the old ideas:
that plants, animals, and humanity
are the boundaries of sense, that it's okay
to draw stars and hoist anchors on Sundays,
or hang in the sky like a cloud of volcanic ash.
But now I know of more cathedral things:
that angels wrap their wings in vintage swimsuits,
that monarchs are best seen from the tops
of trees and, of gingkoes, that their last leaves
leave before the last light leaves.
I'm stupid, right, or maybe even sick?
Is that what you want?
I'd be happy to give it another look.
In the end, it's good if everything seems wrong.
I'm dying, you see, while gesturing toward the beach.
I've given you everything. Now enter.

COMING OUT OF HYPERSPACE INTO THE REMAINS OF ALDERAAN

This is the hour when Chevys head home,
when girls get stoned on abandoned trampolines
and boys order creatine and download porn.

Once upon a time I rolled away the stone, kissed
the broken wings of windowpane birds, lit red lamps
and studied gray smoke for signs of *be* or *believe*.

Now I shiver in the wind, fidget with a twig, wait
for day's last light to leave the tips of leafless trees.
In my bag is a tool to begin the being forgotten.

When this is it, the problem is what to think.
The doctor once asked me what I wanted in my dreams.
A castle in the forest? Eyes the color of sunrise?

No, I said, I want to be rid of the moth that lives
in my mouth. She flies out at night, creeps in at dawn,
dusty and reeking of streetlight. She hides in my throat,

out of sight, but I feel her feathery antennae quiver.
That's why I often cough, cover my mouth when forced
to laugh, or study the sidewalks when I need to talk.

The moth's been seen just once, not by me
but by a homeless woman who lived on the streets
of Memphis, TN. She clutched a broken baby monitor

to her head, unable to aid the child only she could hear.
When I offered to buy her something to eat, she said
I see her wings and then refused my money.

God presses a tired ear against the world. Clouds
flare up into glowing orange coals. I open my mouth
and the choir of a thousand garage doors sings.

The Late Cretaceous

The pills might make me happy,
even if only in the way that a picture of a house is a house.
Still, a picture of a house is better than nothing
and might even begin to seem like the real thing
if inhabited long enough.
Besides, if pills can erase the sadness,
then maybe it too is unreal.

These thoughts weakened his resistance,
which was based on a belief that misery
is a fitting response to fundamental facts about the world—
that what he suffered from was not disease,
but rather an authentic despair that,
though painful and incapacitating,
was morally superior to a drug-induced contentment.
His dilemma, in brief, was this:
if he took the pills, he might lose his identity,
but if he didn't take the pills, he might take his life.
In the end, he concluded it was wiser
to become a simulacrum of himself
than end it altogether.

*

The pills worked, in their way, except
his newfound semi-tranquility was mixed
with a growing suspicion
that no emotions are authentic
in the sense of being required by their object,
and that what explains one's mood is not the operation
of some spiritual-moral-aesthetic sense, but chemical cause and effect.
Not that this bothered him very much.
The pills ensured that.
Plus, if the theory were correct, he should feel,
insofar as he could, whatever would be in his best interests to feel.
So instead of getting depressed, he watched TV,
mostly PBS, especially documentaries about dinosaurs.
Prior to taking meds, a story ending with mass extinction
would have sent him down the drain,
but the absurdity that beasts
as magnificent and globally dominant as these
could be wiped out by a very large rock
now struck him as merely comical.
And if this reversal of affect seemed lamentable,
as it occasionally did,
he would remind himself that natural facts
demand no specific emotional response—
that laughing at what happened to the dinosaurs
is neither more nor less appropriate than weeping.

But sometimes, deep down, where the pills hadn't yet reached,
a nagging voice told him he was lying to himself.
This dissonance caused him some distress.
He reported the voice to his doctor,
a balding, soft-spoken man in his early 50s,
who nodded sympathetically and increased the dosage.

*

As a philosophical experiment,
Descartes placed a ball of beeswax near a flame
and observed that, despite the resulting changes
in its temperature, color, odor, and shape,
the wax remained numerically the same.
Just one thing all along!
To account for this, he proposed that the wax,
indeed any substance, has an essence,
and that this essence can survive various gains and losses
in the substance's outward properties.

*

He wasn't sure when the metamorphosis began.
Maybe there was no specific date.
It started, perhaps, with the gradual loss of his desire

for meat. Other changes followed:
the transformation of his skin into something elephantine,
his lips ossifying and curling into a beak,
the emergence of horns and a bony frill,
his arms thickening into a second pair of legs.
His friends and colleagues didn't seem to notice,
and if they did, they weren't concerned,
and if they were, he wouldn't have cared.
He greeted his alterations with indifference.
His world had flattened out, the deep down voice
gone quiet, his concerns reduced to two:
(i) seek palms, cycads, and ferns;
(ii) avoid T. Rex.

*

Approximately 66 million years ago, an asteroid
between six and fifty miles in diameter crashed
into the Gulf of Mexico just north of Yucatan Peninsula
at a speed of 40,000 mph, creating the Chicxulub Crater,
93 miles in diameter and 12 miles deep. The energy
released by the impact was equivalent to the detonation
of 20 to 900 billion atomic bombs. Within a 600-mile radius,
every living thing was instantly killed. A mega-tsunami
over 300 feet high overwhelmed the western coast of Florida.

A gargantuan plume of dust and rock saturated and darkened the Earth's atmosphere, causing a sudden, long-lasting drop in global temperatures. Within a period of ten years, 75% of all dinosaur species were extinct, including Triceratops, which had roamed the subtropical forests along the inland sea of what's now North America, one of the regions hardest hit.

*

From *Wikipedia*:

> The taxon 'Dinosauria' was formally named in 1841 by paleontologist Sir Richard Owen, who used it to refer to the "distinct tribe or sub-order of Saurian Reptiles" that were then being recognized in England and around the world. The term is derived from Ancient Greek δεινός *(deinos)*, meaning 'terrible, potent or fearfully great', and σαῦρος *(sauros)*, meaning 'lizard or reptile'. Though the taxonomic name has often been interpreted as a reference to dinosaurs' teeth, claws, and other fearsome characteristics, Owen intended it merely to evoke their size and majesty.

*

Even before he could read, Owen was fascinated by them.
He'd spend hours alone, nestled in a beanbag on the living room floor,
paging backwards and forwards through *The Big Picture Book of Dinosaurs*.
Thus, he was delighted when, for his fifth birthday,
he received a stuffed triceratops, half the size of a football,
its body a glossy grey fuzz, the horns snow-white and soft,
the tawny frill a stiffened velveteen.
He carried it with him everywhere he could.
When strangers would ask its name, he wouldn't say—
not because of his extreme shyness,
but because he called it *Owen*,
and the reactions of his older siblings
taught him to be embarrassed by that christening.
That summer, the family vacationed on the Gulf of Mexico,
where Owen enjoyed the shade of his mother's beach umbrella,
and, in the cool white sand, constructed a system of caves
where triceratops found shelter from seagull pterodactyls.
Owen was frequently encouraged to swim, but feared
the crashing waves. Finally he consented, on two conditions:
that he be placed on a raft, and that mom and triceratops join him.
And so it happened that Owen and his mother,
who held triceratops above her head, entered the early morning surf.
Just a few feet in, Owen's mother screamed.
Later on, he would understand that his mother stepped on a stingray,
that the stingray stabbed her ankle, that the sudden, scorching pain
was why she dropped neck-deep to her knees, weeping in the waves,
and why triceratops was lost at sea.

*

Immanuel Kant, *Lectures on Ethics*:

> So far as animals are concerned, we have no direct duties. Animals are not self-conscious and are there merely as a means to an end. That end is man. We can ask, "Why do animals exist?" But to ask, "Why does man exist?" is a meaningless question. If a man shoots his dog because the animal is no longer capable of service, he does not fail in his duty to the dog, because the dog cannot judge.

Please write a 1000-word essay that addresses *one* of the following questions:

1. What if the man who shoots the dog is Owen's mother?
2. What if the dog is triceratops?
3. What if, instead of shooting triceratops, Owen's mother allows it to drown?
4. What if, viewed in one way, triceratops is a stuffed animal, neither alive nor dead and thus incapable of drowning, but, viewed in another way, triceratops is, or is a vital extension of, Owen?
5. Must an entity have the capacity of judgment in order to be morally considerable?
6. Is it true that "Why does man exist?" is a meaningless question?
7. How would Kant's moral philosophy regard a creature both man and beast, both living and extinct?
8. Is it true that Owen, then and now, needs to lighten the fuck up?

*

According to one theory in the literature,
the meaningfulness of any human life
can be understood as the literary merit
of that life's corresponding narrative.
Put another way, your life is meaningful
insofar as your life story is a "good" one.
This, of course, raises more questions
than it answers. Perhaps the most obvious:
What, if anything, makes a narrative good?
If you saw the original *Jurassic Park*
(S. Spielberg, Universal Studios, 1993),
you might remember how it ends:
T. Rex bursts into the Visitors' Center
and unwittingly saves the human beings
who otherwise would have been killed
by the raptors hungrily pursuing them.
(T. Rex attacks and eats the raptors,
thus allowing the human beings to flee.)
This is an example of *deus ex machina*,
a literary device that, according to theorists
going all the way back to Aristotle,
violates the principles of good narration
and therefore ought to be avoided.

*

Ludwig Wittgenstein, *Philosophical Investigations*:

If a ~~lion~~ triceratops could speak, we could not understand him.

*

Instructions for Final Exam:

Construct a narrative (or a life) in which triceratops speaks and is understood.

Toys

They come for Christmas
Explained and unexplained,
Wild games

Taking half the space,
Threads from butterflies,
Miniature airplanes that crash

When unwrapped. We will not
Let them rest or let the flag vibrate
Blue-blue like a cathead.

Weeks we have passed
In out-of-stock stores
(Dollar General, Best Buy, etc.)

Because this trip slices
Everything, red or green,
Too thinly.

Historic ancient land,
Mountain of free will
Surmounted by a tinsel star,

The human heart a little
High-tech fetish.
The robot preens like a cat

In this cheap fun
Virtual world in front of you,
Booboo. Now, sit down

Next to silvery plastic
And imagine a world called water.
You're ready.

Close your little hand.

GOD'S GRANDEUR

The globe is full of beauty
Glowing in the light of moving frames
Collecting moisture and variously charged particles.
Why not admire it?
Decades have passed since I walked away,
Bled, tingled, dabbled in micro-epiphanies,
Explored and mingled my scent with the earth.
There is no nudity without shoes and socks.

Yes, I abused every substance. Guess what?
There's a kernel of nothingness deep in each thing.
And tonight, near the lake, sliver of moon a scythe,
Everything written and the rope just right,
I'll learn that the soul, as it slips through the noose,
Beholds the bright angel's *ah!* dark wings.

I Dreamt I Was at a Dinner Party with Robert Hass

It was late July. We sipped chilled white wine on a stone patio
overlooking a golf course, which itself overlooked a green valley.
I was complaining to Bob that I'd run out of things to write about.
"You're a damn fool," Bob said, which struck me as rather harsh,
especially coming from a man wearing baggy shorts and a t-shirt
at a dinner party. "Write about the condensation on that glass,"
he suggested, pointing to my Pinot Gris, "or the golf course grass,"
gesturing at the grass, and then, with a dramatic sweep of his arm,
"or the golf course generally. There's a book of poems right there.
Open with one about the pro shop, the Astroturf carpeting, the row
of putters on the wall, those teensy pencils, the humongous fishbowl
filled with second-hand golf balls for sale next to the cash register.
There could be a poem for every hole on the golf course, poems
that describe the distinctive features and difficulties of each—
the deceptively tricky par-threes, the dog-legs, the water obstacles—
not to mention poems about the other golfers you might meet.
And that's just sticking to the golf course. You could veer off
in infinitely many directions. Golf balls, after all, are a type of ball,
and balls are spheres, and the Earth is a sphere, as are all planets
and stars, and this would make it natural, even logical, for a poem
about the 9th hole to open up into an epic about the universe."

The dinner bell rang. This was to be a buffet. I followed Bob
to the long table on which a dozen chafing dishes were arranged.
He helped himself to a little bit, sometimes a lot, from each dish,
so that, when we reached the end of the line, Bob's plate overflowed

with a sampling, casually yet artfully arranged, of everything on offer.
When we took our seats with the other guests, Bob spoke with ease
on a dizzying array of subjects, from Hegelian phenomenology
to the mating habits of ostriches to the quality of light on the water
of a Finnish harbor so remote that not even the Finn at our table
had been there. By this time, I had drunk several glasses of wine.
I noticed that if I closed my left eye and stared at Bob with my right,
he appeared to be wearing a halo, but that if I closed my right eye
and studied him with my left, I detected a pair of nubby horns
behind his hairline. Using both of my eyes, Bob began to look
more and more like Socrates. And that's when I started to cry.

Maybe it was because, several years ago, I abandoned philosophy
for poetry, and now I felt as though poetry had abandoned me,
yet there sat Bob, contentedly munching a radish, holding forth,
being both Socrates and one of the great poets of his generation.
Whatever it was, I began to weep—a few restrained tears at first,
but soon they cascaded down my face, not the normal quantity,
but a torrent, as if an ocean had been bottled up inside me,
and the fluid, instead of clear, was the color of blackberries.
My purple tears flooded the room. People began to scream.

Suddenly it was just Bob and me, no longer in the dining room
but in a rowboat at midnight on the open sea. The moon and stars
shone brightly, and I could see golf balls bobbing in the water.
"You worry too much," Bob whispered, "not just about poetry,

but everything else. Why are you so unhappy, always ruminating
on death and your worthless self? Isn't it amazing to be alive, picking
peaches in the orchard, or watching aspens tremble in the breeze?"
"Yes," I whispered back, "I want to be in love with those things,
and sometimes I sort of am, but the sadness always comes back."

Bob fell silent for a long time, his thick arms working the oars,
but then he began to invent, and very softly to recite, a poem
made up entirely of titles of poems by Wallace Stevens.

The men that are falling,
men made out of words—
two versions of the same poem.

Poem written at morning,
on the road home, looking
across the fields and watching
the birds fly – of bright & blue
birds & the gala of the sun.
The oak leaves are hands.

Life is motion, pieces,
a parochial theme—
long and sluggish lines,
loneliness in Jersey City,
a jumbo poem with rhythms.

The poems of our climate?
A golden woman in a silver mirror,
sad strains of a gay waltz,
a postcard from the volcano.

The pure good of theory—
man carrying thing, debris
of life and mind, snow and stars.
The ultimate poem is abstract.
God is good. It is a beautiful night.

Through the moon- and starlit water, I could see the ocean floor,
but instead of sand and coral and tropical fish, it was the golf course
and green valley from before. As Bob rowed, the valley below gave way
to the coast near Sausalito, the marshes of Palo Alto, the bookstores
of Berkeley, then Olema and its apple trees, the trails above Lake Tahoe,
the wooded hills of upstate New York, the snowy streets of Krakow, the
black tiled rooftops of Baekdamsa Temple in South Korea.

The world rolled on beneath the boat, the boat rocking gently
as a cradle. I began drifting off, entering a dream within the dream.
Just before I fell asleep, I asked Bob where we were going.
He said, "I never know," then smiled and kept on rowing.

Among the Rocks

America, brightest smile in the whole wide world,
How do you pick the bones of a dream?

It's simple, really: just pamper your body
And put your head between your knees.

If you love only what's easy for you to love,
Then love and its benefits won't benefit you.

Adversity forces you to improve your brand.
Remember what it said in the in-flight magazine:

Contrary to what you might believe,
The white meat can be saved for pets.

Is the trick in this country to know and yet love?
Give it a try and enjoy the benefits mentioned above!

Low Power Mode

Please pardon the recent history
of our disease, which includes
but is not limited to charm schools,
tanning salons, hamsters in wire cages,
men on the moon, auto-updates,
indicator lights, boner pills, and guns.
The results can be summarized as follows:
missing bodies were not found, oceans
disappeared into the sky, email did not
improve anything, birds became spirits,
horses survived in pictures until the pictures
went up in flames, white flags fluttered
above the cities and small towns,
news travelled underground,
Jesus remained in the tomb,
and the book was closed.

What then?

We gathered at the tumbled wall
between all and thin air
where we wept
and sometimes held each other's hands.

ART THOU PALE FOR WEARINESS

Do you know that I'm weak?
I want to go to heaven and observe the world.
People are people
Except for movie stars.
For instance Matt Damon.
Does he think everyone can be so strong?

The Windhover

He caught the enemy this morning, Black Hawk
   Backed up by a Bell Boeing V-22 Osprey
   In the sunrise of a rebellious dawn.
There is always air combat under the clouds:
Cyclic pitch, rate of ascent, throttle, tail rotor—
    These make him happy! He radios back to get ideas, swings,
    Rolls out, blades easily on the archway, door and glider, resists
Strong winds. His heart is hidden—reach in and grab that thing!

A feast of beauty and glory and cruelty, oh soul, pride, my dove
   Fasten your seatbelt, this hellfire has cost us billions.
One can't help but exclaim, "My love, it's dangerous, oh my love!"

   No surprise, these choppers have laid waste to millions:
Yellow-black songbirds, apartment blocks, and mosques—
   Civilians scattering in infrared visions.

Corona Sutra

The End blew in horses with bat-like wings,
swarms of animated gifs, drifts of human limbs
charred as if roasted on a spit. We dug trenches
in the fields, traded all our ideas for things, stashed elders
in the bellies of B-17s. Nothing that survived
was exactly what it seemed. Trees were not trees, bees
not bees, and the Vs overhead were drones, not geese.

Thus we began to hammer out our slogan.
Finally we settled on *Beef You Can Believe In.* The irony
was lost on everyone but the gargoyles, who lived, as we did,
with scare quotes around their names. For eons we floundered
in a sort of –ish zone, no longer what we'd been, not yet
what we'd become. We needed something suited
to our talents, but not easily transferable to video.

Winter was the toughest time, what with refugees
huddled around their fires, confusing that feeble light
with the illumination we had to offer. On the bleakest days
we felt like nincompoops, trudging through the snow
past boarded-up shops, our sleds piled high with gilded tomes.

You didn't mean to be such a tough crowd.
It's hard to get a creature to shed its protective layer.
The trick was convincing you that an exoskeleton
does more harm than good. (Imagine how that went.)

Sometimes we'd break through. Your shell would crack
like lake ice, offering a glimpse of swirling darkness
underneath—but deeper, beyond that darkness,
we could always see a light. It was just too cold.
A week later and you'd be frozen over again.

Could it be that you are more like fields
than frozen lakes, sown and reaped according to seasons
of your own, best by your own hands? We piled our gifts
on makeshift tables, let you wander by as you wished.
Our powers atrophied. It felt good to let them go.

Gradually, something like the world returned.
We learned to be content just to be here among you—
hearing you laugh or sing softly to yourself, watching you
hang clean sheets in the sun, or drifting off with the paper
in your lap, forgetful of what has been and what again will be,
drunk on the flutter of the ginkgo's golden wings.

I Am Gone Out

I am gone out, gone cold,
nothing but bones, veneer
of onionskin, thin

as no good thing is ever thin.
A bump, a brush, a mere
breath would do me in.

Please have the decency
not to stare at me directly.
Use that mirror there,

the ivory-handled glass.
Stand six feet away from me.
Make tight your mask.

There. Now you've seen
what I've become: withered tree,
hollow space between

the lid and foot
of an urn, foam on the sea
of being and of been.

Dig the ditch. Inscribe
the stone. Come spring I'll be
the green beneath your boot.

Pink Salt

Everyone knows what's coming:
advancing seas, the collapse of coastal cities,
hundreds of millions of refugees.

This doesn't stop him from waiting
in a long line of air-conditioned vehicles
for his turn at the Shammy Shine,

then driving to Costco, six miles
out of town, just to satisfy a craving
for pink Himalayan-salted almonds.

He doesn't know pink salt is mined
in the Punjab region of Pakistan,
well south of the Himalayan peaks,

or that Pakistan has Karachi,
the world's fifth most-populous city,
clinging to the coast of the Arabian Sea.

Nor does he imagine the raging fad for salt—
pink, Celtic, smoked, Black Hawaiian—
might be understood

as the collective unconscious
expressing, in the marketplace, its awareness
of the soon-to-be ubiquity of brine.

Equitum Tres Coloratum

The clouds above this town rain bones
while children hunker in their caves of dirt.
Outside each house, a black flag waves,
but black now comes in many colors.
Down in the garden, we unearth a horse,
a rearing mustang made of matter

and form, in Aristotle's terms. The matter
is solid plastic—no blood, no bones,
no heart, certainly not the size of a horse.
At five inches tall, it's a toy in the dirt.
We rub it clean to reveal the colors:
white, brown, and black. We feel waves

of memory, or what seem like waves,
but might be particles of matter,
atoms devoid of tastes and colors.
We huddle in the garden shed as bones
like spears strike the freshly plowed dirt.
We swap ancient stories about the horse:

the wooden one of Troy; Siddhartha's horse,
Kanthaka; the steeds that ride the waves
of the apocalypse. Down in the dirt,
our children wonder what's the matter
with the weather these days. Are the bones
a sign of something, they ask, like the colors

of our flags? We can't explain those colors
or the meaning of the weather. The horse
gets passed around as we pray for the bones
to cease, but the clouds come on in waves,
releasing femurs, clavicles, ossified matter
of all sorts, pounding our crops into the dirt.

The children are quiet in their caves of dirt.
A girl with a box of crayons colors
every picture black in her matter-
of-fact way, including a winged horse.
A trembling boy peeks out from the cave, waves
at his father through the hail of bones.

Does any of it matter? In the end we are bones,
destined for dirt. Yet the boy's father waves,
unfurls his colors, and flies to his son on the plastic horse.

THIS BAG IS NOT A TOY

Punching bags, laundry bags, bags on planes
for puke. Bags of money and bags of dicks,
dicks just bags of bad blood. Sandbags damming
the rising sea, the sea a simmering stew of bags.
Diaper bags, colostomy bags, a man teabagging
his blowup bag. Bags of transmuting and bags
of need, bags of devouring and bags of weed.
Grocery bags crammed with Family Size bags,
book bags bulging with guns but no books,
golf bags for Presidents, body bags for troops.
When the angels come, transparent and small,
we'll mistake them for Ziploc sandwich bags.
They'll weep for us after seeing such things.
In the gutter, a bag of barbecued wings.

November

The snow comes down, accumulates
in drifts, meringues, white cliffs that overhang
and cling to roofs. The universal

is abstract, yet you are a particular,
your hallway closet stocked with shoes
and wool coats. Once, flying above

the clouds and a patchwork earth, you occupied
a point between these two: yourself, where everything
is hugely you, and the annihilating view

from Pluto. From that midway space,
you saw and felt your place, soul-sized and true,
in the starry plate's eternal swirl:

self beyond self but still itself, half-heavened,
reflected in the glass, sipping water
and eating peanuts from a tiny foil pack.

Life post-epiphany is lived like pre-.
The usual errands at the same old shops,
everything unchanged—all except the snow

beyond the window, low clouds now,
drifts from which children build separate men
the sun will melt into one.

Gingerbread Man

My gingerbread man says drink it
if it gives you shield, says remember
the nearest exit might be behind you,
says you're probably part of God
and love won't let you go back.

Used to be I had only three emotions:
Emergency Cone,
Crow Atop Utility Pole,
and Discarded Doll Stuck In Storm Drain—
but gingerbread man got me past all that.

Now I have more feelings than I know
what to do with. And when the elevator
is packed with rotting mummies,
gingerbread man covers my eyes
and sings me a nonsense lullaby.

Sometimes, when I'm feeling shy,
I hide with gingerbread man in the attic,
up there with all the mounted deer heads
and fading daguerreotypes
of nineteenth century clerics—

but gingerbread man never cries.
If he did, the tears would ruin
his Red Hots eyes, which he needs
in order to see the world in his sweet
and round and ruby way.

It's the only world worth knowing.
Where else can you get a haircut, fill up
the truck, and mail a couple of love letters?
This one's for my gingerbread man.
The other is meant for you.

Poem Written in My Favorite Coffee Shop after Discussing Plato's *Symposium* with Undergraduates

I come here nearly every day
to hide, write, and fill up the tank.
No special ops, no caring about knowing.
Just check out all the love arriving!
Poems from the trash decorate
the walls of this place.
The doorways are draped
in the most amazingly cheerful chili lights.
Everyone rejoices in God, who,
at this time of year, is nothing
but a seat near the fire and feeling
that beauty is this world,
beauty's waves the sea,
the beautiful always being
and always becoming beauty.

Four Proofs Wherein Teeth are Demonstrated to Be the Soul

#1
there's a massive temple in Sri Lanka built
to house a Buddha tooth FYI
it's not the only shrine devoted
to a Buddha tooth (there's five more including
one in Rosemead, CA) & while some say
worshipping a tooth is weird
it sort of makes sense
if teeth are the soul

#2
if you die in a plane crash or fire or whatever
and your corpse is destroyed or totally
unrecognizable
they'll still find you
if they find your teeth because
teeth are your essence & survive destruction
of the body (hello?)

#3
teeth are not words
or food but everything
you say or eat passes over them
kind of like a river over rocks
and rocks endure
basically forever

#4
last but not least how about the love
you shower on those babies, brushing/flossing etc., like
the concern you're supposed to show for your
soul & let's not forget the obsession
with whitening (how soul is *that*?)
or the fact of the dentist's clean white
coat and her silently judging your teeth with that blinding
bright light behind her head like
you guessed it
God

DAYSHIFT AT THE PLACE OF SAFEKEEPING

Flowers heat up in a truck
at the edge of the cemetery.
A hairdo in the parking lot
looks like Easter basket grass.

I can't deliver another wreath
to the tent. It's impossible
to communicate with grievers.
Victory doesn't feel like this.

Still, "Have a good one" and
"It is what it is" would be
totally inappropriate.
What is anything anyway?

We are not dust.
We are not children.
We are not God's creatures.
We are not going home.

Rivers flow into the ocean?
Big deal. Slumped in a chair
on the Astroturf fringe,
an old man sleeps like a baby.

THE END

Not everyone knew what to say.
(Click here if the ship has gone down.)
Time swallowed our secret treasures.
Some of us knew they would never come back.

When the sun disappeared, the lights came on.
Cat videos were among the most popular.
Some of us were not sure what was going on.
Weight loss followed irritability and fatigue.

The formula was simple and memorable:
When we showed up, the birds flew away.
By then, everyone knew more or less what to expect.
It was dark when the ship went down. Then it was over.

Fantasy Hymn

Life is wonderful, y'all! I shouldn't say that
but when the sun shines in search of the sea
this gig seems brilliant.
My mama told me when I was younger
"Obie, if you confess your sins
it means you're not

the Other." Okay, but not right now.
I'll keep my material inside because I'm tired.
I was, after all, born human.
Books, especially this one, defy me
while the TV squawks of stolen elections & coups
hotter than Myanmar chilies.

I used to enjoy fantastic acting,
jagged rocks, and clouds of weed
but now, somehow, I've managed
to haul my ragged ass from the sea—
to the mountains—to the sun—
above, dear mama, me.

Another Summer

Because the drive is long,
and because our phones
are nearly out of juice, my wife,
who is fond of making lists,
starts a running tab of roadkill.

Six deer in total,
six and a half if you count
the decapitated buck, plus
three raccoons, two possums,
one reeking skunk,

and Robert Lowell
in the trunk, packed in my suitcase,
sandwiched between swimsuits
and the toiletry kit, his chin
at rest on a Brahmin hand.

After we arrive, and several glasses
of white wine, my sister sticks
our catalog of mangled casualties
to the door of her fridge, alongside
family photographs and heirloom recipes.

Lowell, parked on a nightstand
in the guest room, is ignored all week.
At night, he watches my wife and me
read magazines and try, once or twice,
to have noiseless sex.

Every family is as old as Lowell's.
Each has a pedigree that begins
with the origins of humankind—
tamers of fire who worshipped the sky,
carvers of the first and holiest verse.

During the days, through windows
that open onto the lake, Lowell listens
to the sounds this family makes—
splashing, squabbling, swamping the canoe,
cracking open cans of low-calorie beer.

On the highway home, new carrion
has replaced the old. We talk and laugh
about moments from our visit.
From the guest room of my sister's house,
Robert Lowell begins to miss us.

Epilogue

Connections and huge bonuses—
why don't you help me now
that I want to work
with borrowings from what y'all were dreaming?
I hear the voice:
The artist's eyes are not your eyes.
I turn on the flashlight and shake it.
Sometimes I write
with a technique that bewilders my sight.
The results look like pictures
of a wild pig named Pete.
Growing up white,
bullshit was easily canonized.
All is not well.
Why not tell what happened
and pray for mercy?
Vermeer's soft light
illuminates bad maps
and long forgotten women,
yet still we give awesome
attention to figures
in pictures painted by
he/him/his.

About the Author

Old phones, broken bones, rundown hometowns,
the sore throats of our lovesick souls, the autumn birds
of inscrutable desire. Those were difficult times in our lives.

Keeping the lawns low and precisely edged was required.
We tried to sing as best we could, which wasn't much fun,
but it was thought to protect us from brain damage.

Still, the birdsongs meant nothing, no matter how long
or how earnestly we listened. Then why did we listen?
Maybe we were looking for a decent place to hide.

We stumbled upon the fact that the human mind,
though difficult to find, is connected to the body.
We let the grass grow, our hearts fill up with rain,

and as our livestock fattened on acorns and grapes,
it seemed that the prayers we'd scribbled in the margins
of our books were finally being answered by God.

The birdsongs began to make sense. Something about
carrying, bending, turning, stretching, breathing, climbing.
Something about our lives being palaces of light.

Notes

"In the Credit Union Lobby" draws from a *Field & Stream* article entitled "Kentucky Deer Hunter with Two Prosthetic Arms Takes a Massive 10 Pointer", first published May 3, 2019.

"Mark 6:11" alludes to this verse from the Gospel of Mark: "And whosoever shall not receive you, nor hear you, when ye depart thence, shake off the dust under your feet for a testimony against them."

"Heart of Hearts" mentions Sèvres, which is a suburb of Paris and home to the International Prototype Meter.

After

Many poems in this section are "after" poems by other authors. In most cases, the source poem is indicated by the title: "God's Grandeur" and "The Windhover" by Gerard Manley Hopkins, "Among the Rocks" by Robert Browning, "Art Thou Pale for Weariness" by Percy Bysshe Shelley, "The End" by Mark Strand, and "Epilogue" by Robert Lowell. The two exceptions are "Toys" and "Fantasy Hymn", which are after Sylvia Plath's "Balloons" and John Berryman's "Dream Song #14", respectively.

The italicized poem within "I Dreamt I Was at a Dinner Party with Robert Hass" is, as the poem itself indicates, made entirely of titles of poems by Wallace Stevens – but I assembled it, not Robert Hass.

Acknowledgments

Grateful acknowledgment goes to the editors and staffs of journals in which versions of these poems first appeared:

$ (Poetry is Currency): "The Host Will Let You In Soon" and "Low Power Mode"
32 Poems: "Sonnet to My Inheritance"
Alaska Quarterly Review: "Gingerbread Man"
Bennington Review: "Ricketts Creek"
Birmingham Poetry Review: "Bushkill Creek"
Boulevard: "Pink Salt"
Copper Nickel: "Coming Out of Hyperspace into the Remains of Alderaan"
Crab Creek Review: "Craters," "Fragments from the Gumball Scrolls" and "Portrait of Woman with Cabbages"
Florida Review: "Blood Vessels", "Jaws" and "Reunion"
The Greensboro Review: "Vending Machine Sutra"
Lake Effect: "Meditation for Beginners"
Mississippi Review: "Eagle Beach"
New Ohio Review: "Blue Camaro" and "Thief"
North American Review: "Sonnet on My Birthday"
Passages North: "Equitum Tres Coloratum"
Poetry Northwest: "November"
Raleigh Review: "Dayshift at the Place of Safekeeping"
Quiddity: "I Am Gone Out" and "Saturday Morning"
Rhino: "Mark 6:11" and "The Owen McLeod Poet Action Figure"
Salt Hill: "Another Summer"

The Shore: "Corona Sutra" and "Entomology"

Sixth Finch: "I Dreamt I Was at a Dinner Party with Robert Hass" and "The Late Cretaceous"

Smartish Pace: "About the Author" and "How to Stop Yourself from Crying"

Southern Poetry Review: "Black Box," "Heart of Hearts" and "Yet Another Walk Away"

The Southern Review: "In the Credit Union Lobby"

Sugar House Review: "My Life in Oz"

The Sun: "Last Requests"

UCity Review: "Among the Rocks," "Art Thou Pale for Weariness," "Epilogue," "God's Grandeur," "Toys" and "The Windhover"

Willow Springs: "This Bag Is Not a Toy"

Yale Review: "Breakup at the Starfish Brasserie"

Yemassee: "Four Proofs Wherein Teeth are Demonstrated to Be the Soul"

About the Author

Owen McLeod's debut collection, *Dream Kitchen,* won the Vassar Miller Prize in Poetry. His poems appear in *Copper Nickel, Massachusetts Review, Missouri Review, New England Review, Ploughshares, The Southern Review* and elsewhere, and his work has been supported by a Walter E. Dakin Fellowship from the Sewanee Writers' Conference. He is a professor of philosophy at Lafayette College in Easton, Pennsylvania.

Also by Owen McLeod

Dream Kitchen (University of North Texas Press, 2019),
Winner of the Vassar Miller Prize in Poetry

Before After is printed in Adobe Caslon
www.saturnaliabooks.org